to My Moon
Bound Girl,

_____

from _____

with love to the moon and back

Moon Bound Girl
Melody's Music

Created & Illustrated by
Leigh Ann Agee

★

Written by Dave Dunseath

Moon Bound Girl
Bristol, Tennessee

For my loving parents,
who forever encourage and support
this Moon Bound Girl to chase her
dreams and follow her heart.

~la

ISBN 978-0-578-14327-9

Moon Bound Girl

Moon Bound Girl
P.O. Box 683
Bristol, TN 37621-0683
www.moonboundgirl.com

Printed in China
10 9 8 7 6 5 4 3
Mfg. DSC
Shenzhen, China
November 2016/Q14003761-3

My name is *Melody* and I'm a Moon Bound Girl

Once upon a time

I discovered something marvelous
I found I have the potential
To fill the world with awesomeness

Make ordinary moments
Extraordinarily magical
And anything unthinkable
Suddenly imaginable

So, I imagined a world
The way I wanted it to be
And the first thing I changed . . .
Was me

What a revelation
For a pretty shy girl
To know I have the power
To change the world

Overcome obstacles
Face the impossible
Brave what is deemed
Completely improbable

Laugh when I'm told
It's beyond inconceivable
Far-fetched, ridiculous
Believed unbelievable

That's when it happened
That's how I knew
I was a girl
Bound for the moon

And one by one
My fears disappeared
While breath-taking, hair-raising
Ideas appeared

Now I'm wishing upon stars
And chasing my dreams
Only I know which ones
Are meant just for me

For I was born
To leap without a net
Never look down
Or look back with regret

I'm gonna march and sing
To a different drummer
And wonder about worlds
I've yet to discover

I'm just like you
I'm an ordinary girl
Who realized it's possible
To take on the world

With courage and grit
Wisdom and wit
I'm persistent when others
Persistently quit

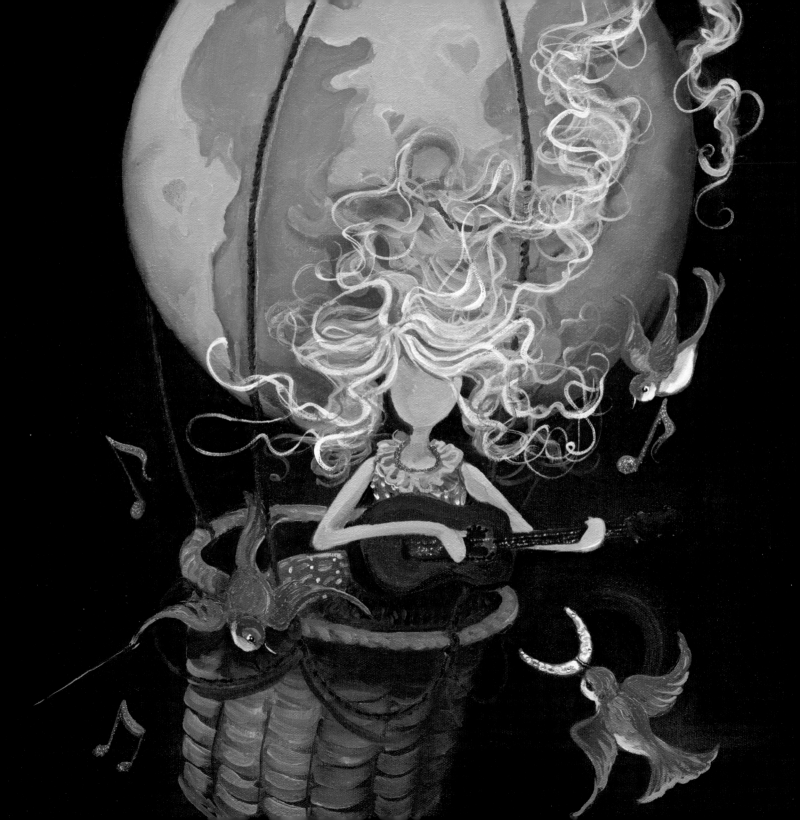

I look to my dreams
For inspiration
'Cause I can go anywhere
With my imagination

There are so many things
Us girls are made of
Sweetness and light
Goodness and love

We're strong-willed and caring
Giving, kind-hearted
We're plucky and spunky
Oh I'm just getting started

Makes a girl wonder
Who wrote the rules
Deciding what dreamers
Can and can't do?

Can't be done, won't be done
Don't try and shouldn't
Aren't those excuses
From those who couldn't?

I still fall down
Have moments of doubt
I either accept failure
Or figure it out

Maybe I'm a little stubborn
Or just can't resist
Doing what others
Would never risk

Nincompoops, naysayers
Are all doom and gloom
They say I've been blinded
By the light of the moon

It's too far, too risky
It's too great a fall
You'll get burned for trying
So why try at all?

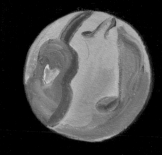

Ha, maybe they're right
I hate to admit it
'Cause the moon's getting brighter
Every minute *I'm in it*

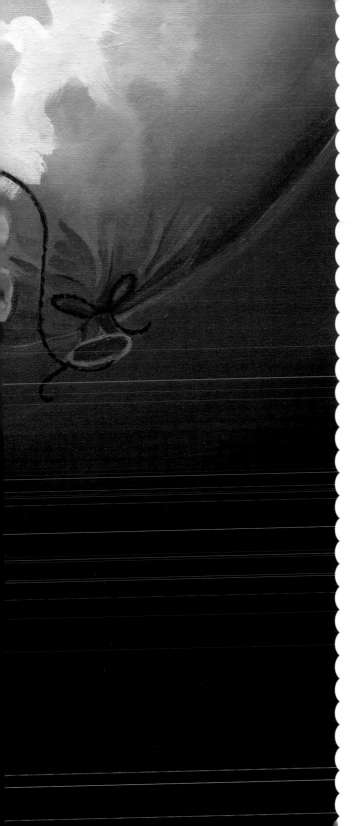

I'm alive for a reason
To follow my passion
So I can be the girl
I've always imagined

Writing and singing
Playing my songs
Finding a world
Where I know I belong

Though I never imagined
Doing something I love
Would make my hair do
What hair never does

It hangs in the air
As if it had wings
When I'm playing the songs
I love to sing

I know it looks crazy
Twisting and swirling
Dancing with butterflies
Weaving and curling

But it isn't the wind
That makes it all messy
And bungled and jumbled
Like tangled spaghetti

My hair only rises
The moment I start
To chase my dreams
And follow my heart

So if all you see
Is a tangled disaster
Then maybe you haven't yet
Found what you're after

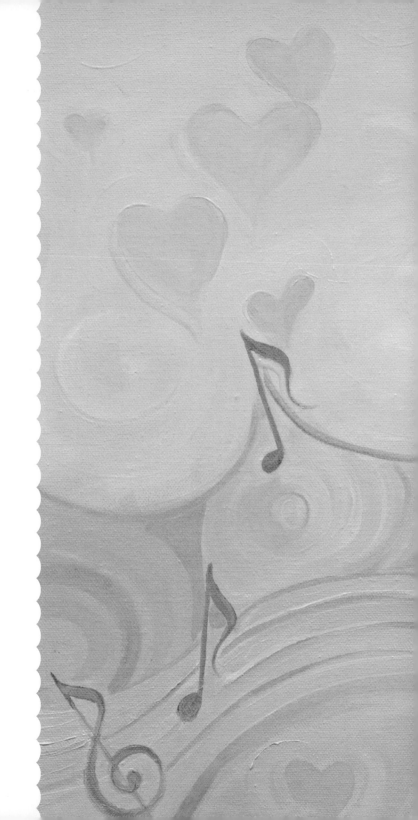

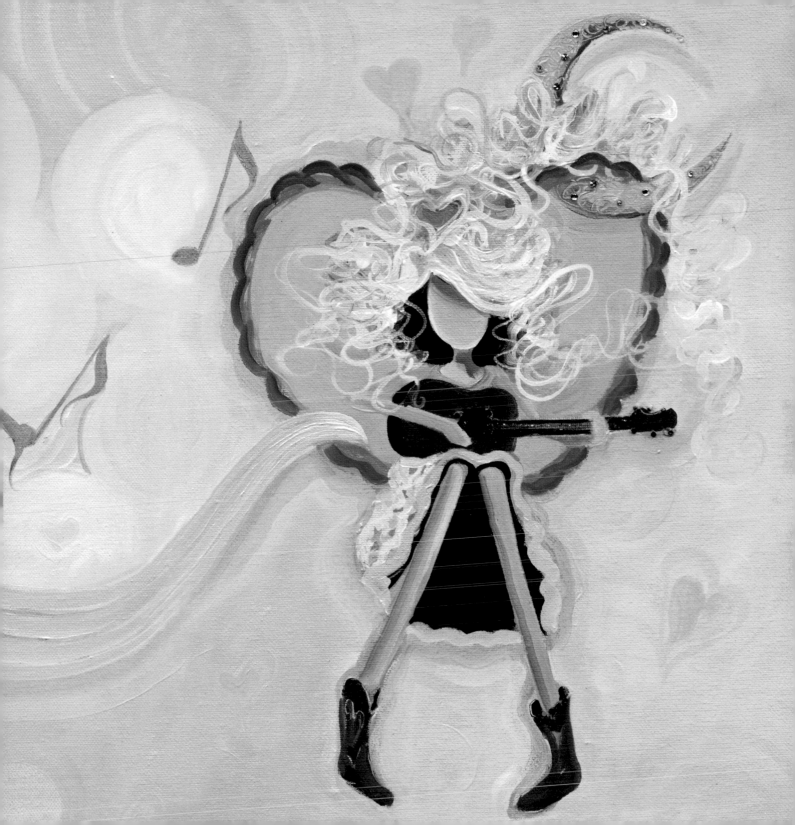

My name is *Melody*

and I'm bound for the moon . . .
And it can happen to you
If you believe too . . .

If you believe…

You are a
Moon
Bound Girl too!

What do you love to do that makes your hair stand on end?

_____

_____

_____

_____

_____

Your biggest dream is _____

_____

_____

You're most passionate about _____

_____

You get butterflies when _____

_____

You're happiest when _____

_____

_____

You believe in yourself because _____

_____

_____

Dreams are life-long journeys
so don't lose heart too soon
Never give up and never stop
shooting for the moon

Melody

Moon
Bound
Girl

www.moonboundgirl.com

Hey, you just
gotta believe...